Contents

Written by
David Clayton

Illustrated by
Peter Richardson

Series editor **Dee Reid**

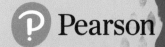
Pearson

Characters

Joe

Man in a dark suit

Tricky words

- restricted
- signs
- everywhere
- dome
- anything
- spacesuit
- breathe
- forced

Read these words to the student. Help them with these words when they appear in the text.

Introduction

Joe knew there was something strange going on in Moon City but he didn't know what. There were 'Red Zone Restricted Area' signs everywhere. He had an idea – if he could get out on to the dome he could see what was going on in the whole city. But he would need a spacesuit and he knew that going out on the dome would be dangerous.

Panic in Space

Joe was busy trying to work things out.
Something strange was going on in Moon City
but he didn't know what. There were
'Red Zone Restricted Area' signs everywhere.
I don't know what those signs mean, thought
Joe, *but I'm going to find out!*

Joe looked up at the huge dome that covered Moon City. All around the outside of the dome were metal platforms with ladders going up and down between them. The ladders were quick exits in case anything went wrong in the city.

As Joe looked up he saw a tiny shape on one of the ladders.
What is that person doing up there? he thought.

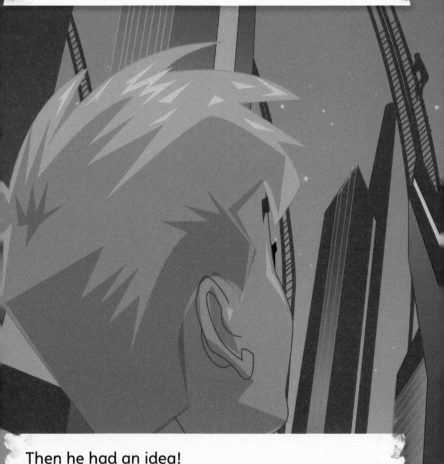

Then he had an idea!
If I could get out on the dome I could see the whole city, even the Red Zones. I could see what's going on! he thought. *But if I'm going outside the dome I will need a spacesuit...*

Joe knew there was a way out to the dome from the science labs. He hung around near the door to the labs. Then, when someone came out, he slipped in. Nobody saw him. He crept into the airlock. He saw some spacesuits hanging up and he put one on.

It was dangerous to go outside the dome and Joe's hands shook as he opened the outer door.
But I've got to find out what's going on, he thought.

Joe started to climb up one of the ladders but his hands were still shaking. If he fell, it was a hundred metre drop to the rocks below! Joe looked up. He thought he could see a dark shape above him on the dome but it was hard to tell.

As Joe climbed, he saw strange flashes of light far off. *They must be coming from the mines,* he thought. Then he stopped climbing. *There was no way the lights could be coming from the mines. The mines were in the other direction! What is going on?* thought Joe.

As Joe turned to get a better look at the lights his foot slipped off the ladder.

"Aaaah!" he yelled as he slid over the edge of the dome. He hit the platform by the door and tried to grab the ladder but he was falling too fast.

Joe fell down and down.
Then suddenly he was yanked to a stop.
His air tank had caught between two ladders!
He was hanging upside down in midair.
Now what? thought Joe.

Joe managed to grab hold of a ladder and slowly worked himself the right way up.

I must get back inside, Joe thought, *it is too dangerous out here*. He began to pull himself up the ladder, back towards the door. But after a few minutes he had to stop. He was finding it hard to breathe. He looked at his air tank. A red light said 'Low Air'. His tank had been cracked in the fall and he was losing the air he needed to breathe.

Joe tried to keep climbing but he could feel his arms growing weaker.

I'm not going to make it, he thought.

He forced himself to take one step, then another. There were a hundred more above him. He felt dizzy. He tried to hold on to the ladder.

I must not fall! he thought, but he felt so weak.

Joe thought he saw a dark shape just above him. Then everything went black.

Joe woke up lying on the floor inside Moon City. A man in a dark suit was looking down at him. "What were you doing out there?" asked the man. "You passed out and fell. You would have died if I hadn't been there to save you!" "Did you see the strange flashes?" said Joe weakly. "They were from the mines," said the man. "They can't have been," said Joe, "the mines are in the other direction."

"Just go home," said the man. He seemed angry now. "And never go out on the dome again."

As Joe set off home his mind was buzzing.
Why had the man been on the dome?
What were those strange flashes?
Joe had a feeling that something bad was
happening in Moon City...

Quiz ////////////////////////////

Text comprehension

Literal comprehension
p4 Why are there ladders on the outside of the dome?
p14 How did Joe know the flashes were not from the mine?

Inferential comprehension
p7 What is dangerous about going outside the dome?
p11/14 In what ways was Joe lucky?
p13 Why did Joe pass out?

Personal response
- Do you think the man knows what the strange flashes are?
- Do you think Joe is brave or foolish?

Word knowledge

p3 Find a word made of two words.
p9 Which adjective describes the flashes of light?
p10 Find three powerful verbs.

Spelling challenge

Read these words:
everything   towards   different
Now try to spell them!

Ha! Ha! Ha!

How does the man in the moon eat his food?

In satellite dishes!

Find out about

- the planets in our solar system.

Tricky words

- exist
- survive
- breathe
- carbon dioxide
- telescopes
- satellite
- meteors
- asteroids

Read these words to the student. Help them with these words when they appear in the text

Introduction

Earth is one of the eight planets which orbit the Sun.
We call the Sun and the eight planets the Solar System.
Earth is the only planet that has enough water, air, heat and
land for humans to survive.

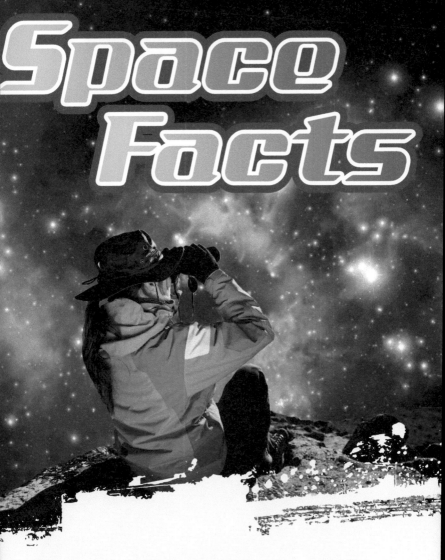

Space Facts

Have you ever looked up into the sky at night?
What did you see?
If it was a clear night you would have seen
the Moon and stars.
But you might have been lucky and
spotted a shooting star.

Sun

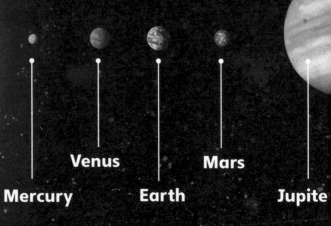

Mercury

Venus

Earth

Mars

Jupite

The Solar System

If you look up into the sky on a clear day you will see the Sun. But be careful, you should never look right at the Sun.

The Earth is one of eight planets which orbit the Sun. We call the Sun and the eight planets the Solar System.

Saturn

Uranus

Neptune

The Sun

The Sun is the star closest to Earth.
It is a giant ball of burning gas.
The light from the Sun takes
eight minutes to reach Earth.
Without the Sun there would
be no life on Earth.

Earth

Earth is the third planet away from the Sun. It is 93 million miles from the Sun. That means Earth gets enough heat and light for human life to exist, but not so much that it is too hot for humans to survive.

Humans need the right amount of water, air, heat and land to survive. Earth is the only planet in the Solar System that has all these things.

Mercury

Could humans live on Mercury?
No!
Mercury is the planet nearest to the Sun.
It is 36 million miles from the Sun.
There is no air on Mercury so humans
could not breathe. In some places on
Mercury it is very hot (427°C)
and in other places it is very cold (-183°C).

Venus

Could humans live on Venus?
No!
Venus is 67 million miles from the Sun.
It is covered in deadly carbon dioxide clouds
and the air pressure is very high.
Humans would not be able to breathe.

Mars

Could humans live on Mars?
No!
Mars is 227 million miles from the
Sun. It has almost no air so humans
would not be able to breathe.
On Mars it is sometimes as hot as
Earth but sometimes much colder.

The other planets in our Solar System are Jupiter, Saturn, Uranus and Neptune. You could not live on these planets because they are just huge balls of freezing gas.

Jupiter

Uranus

Saturn

Neptune

We know about planets because we can see them through telescopes. But did you know you can see Mercury, Venus, Mars, Jupiter and Saturn without a telescope? They just look like really bright stars.

The Stars

You don't need a telescope to see stars
in the night sky but they are a very long way away.
Even if you could fly at a million miles an hour
it would take nearly three thousand years to get there!
Travel to the stars is impossible.
Human life is not long enough.
But even if we cannot **travel** far into Space,
we can **see** a long way into Space.
The Hubble telescope is on a satellite
going round the Earth. It shows us more
of Space than we can see from Earth.

The Moon

The Moon is also in our Solar System.
As the Earth travels around the Sun,
the Moon travels around the Earth.
It spins in time with the Earth so we only
ever see one side of the Moon.
Some scientists think the Moon used to be
part of the Earth. They think that a huge
object hit the Earth. This broke off a piece
of the Earth and that became the Moon.

Meteors

Have you ever seen a flash of
light in the night sky?
Did it look like a shooting star?
It might have been a meteor.
Meteors are bits of asteroids
which burn up and glow
when they enter the
Earth's atmosphere.

Asteroids

Asteroids are rocks that orbit the Sun.
If a large asteroid hit the Earth, it would wipe out
human life. Its dust would block the light of the Sun
and without light, humans could not grow any food.

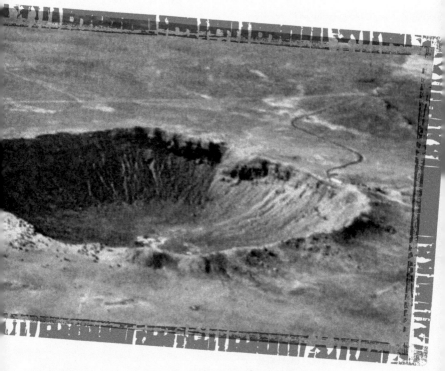

This large crater in America is four times
the size of London! It was made when
a huge asteroid smashed into Earth.
Some scientists think that the dinosaurs
might have been killed when a huge asteroid
hit the Earth.
But don't worry, that won't happen to us!
We can now track asteroids coming towards
the Earth and stop them with rockets.

Text comprehension

Literal comprehension
p23 Why is the Earth the only planet where humans can live?

p31 What made the huge crater in America?

Inferential comprehension
p27 Which two planets can't you see without a telescope?

p29 Why is one side of the moon called 'the dark side'?

p31 Why might an asteroid have killed the dinosaurs?

Personal response
• Do you ever look up into the sky at night?

• Have you ever seen a shooting star?

Word knowledge

p27 Which word joins the two parts of the second sentence in the first box?

p27 Find five words in the word 'planets'.

p28 Find a word that means 'cannot be done'.

Spelling challenge

Read these words:

watched   young   quietly

Now try to spell them!

Ha! Ha! Ha!

What is the centre of gravity?

The letter v!